This book belongs to:

Kaiden O'Brien

➡️ How did the skunk call his mom?

with a smellular phone

➡️ How did the skunk call his mom?

with a smellular phone

➡️

How do you make

a tissue dance?

you put a boogie in it

How do you make

a tissue dance?

you put a boogie in it

What is the soft stuff

between shark's teeth?

A slow swimmer

What is the soft stuff

between shark's teeth?

A slow swimmer

Mommy, can I lick
the bowl?

No, please flush instead

Mommy, can I lick
the bowl?

No, please flush instead

Why do sausages
have bad manners?
They spit in the pan
Why do sausages
have bad manners?
They spit in the pan

What style of tie do

pigs wear?

A pigsty

What style of tie do

pigs wear?

A pigsty

What do you call a
duck who has fangs?
Count Quackula

What do you call a
duck who has fangs?
Count Quackula

What do cats put in
their soft drinks?
Mice cubes

What do cats put in
their soft drinks?
Mice cubes

Why are four legged
animals bad dancers?
They have 2 left feet

Why are four legged
animals bad dancers?
They have 2 left feet

What do you call a
camel with 3 humps?
Humphrey

What do you call a
camel with 3 humps?
Humphrey

What do you call a
penguin in the desert?
Lost
What do you call a
penguin in the desert?
Lost

What is a dog's

favorite food?

Everything you eat

What is a dog's

favorite food

Everything you eat

What do you give a
sick elephant?

A very big paper bag

What do you give a
sick elephant?

A very big paper bag

What do you call an
unwashed elephant?
A smellyphant

What do you call an
unwashed elephant?
A Smellyphant

What's orange and

sounds like a parrot?

A Carrot

What's orange and

sounds like a parrot?

A Carrot

What's black and white
and eats like a horse?
A zebra

What's black and white
and eats like a horse?
A zebra

What do dogs and
trees have in common?
Bark

What do dogs and
trees have in common?
Bark

It takes 3 sheep
to make a sweater...
j/k they can't knit

It takes 3 sheep
to make a sweater...
j/k they can't knit

What would you do if
a bull charged you?
Pay him cash

What would you do if
a bull charged you?
Pay him cash

Why do giraffes have long necks? Their feet are stinky

Why do giraffes have long necks? Their feet are stinky

Where do bees go
when they are sick?
The Waspital

Where do bees go
when they are sick?
The Waspital

What time is it when
you see an alligator?
Time to go
What time is it when
you see an alligator?
Time to go

What do you call a

baby whale?

A little squirt

What do you call a

baby whale?

a little squirt

What animal falls

from the sky?

A raindeer

What animal falls

from the sky?

A raindeer

What do you call a
fly without wings?
A walk

What do you call a
fly without wings?
A walk

When is it unlucky to

see a black cat?

When you're a mouse

When is it unlucky to

see a black cat?

When you're a mouse

What do dalmations

say after dinner?

That hits the spots

What do dalmations

day after dinner?

That hits the spots

Why do birds
fly south?
It's too far to walk

Why do birds
fly south?
It's too far to walk

What do you give a
pig with eczema?
Oinkment

What do you give a
pig with eczema?
Oinkment

What do frogs order

at the drive thru?

French flies

What do frogs order

at the drive thru?

French flies

How did the crab

call his mom?

with a shellular phone

How did the crab

call his mom?

with a shellular phone

What happens when a

cat eats a lemon?

it becomes a sour puss

What happens when a

cat eats a lemon?

it becomes a sour puss

What do you call a
napping bull?
A bulldozer

What do you call a
napping bull?
A bulldozer

What should you give
a dog with a fever?

Ketchup, it's a hot dog

What should you give
a dog with a fever?

Ketchup, it's a hot dog

What do you call

spiders who just married?

Newlywebs

What do you call

spiders who just married?

Newlywebs

How do you make a
baby snake cry?
Take her rattle

How do you make a
baby snake cry?
Take her rattle

Why did the firefly
get good grades?
He was bright

Why did the firefly
get good grades
He was bright

Where do noisy dogs

hangout?

The barking lot

Where do noisy dogs

hangout?

The barking lot

What do you call

a retired fly?

A flew

What do you call

a retired fly?

A flew

Why do lions eat
raw meat?
They can't cook

Why do lions eat
raw meat?
They can't cook

What is the largest

moth in the world?

A Mam-moth

What is the largest

moth in the world?

A Mam-Moth

What should you give

a sick bird?

Tweet-ment

What should you give

a sick bird?

Tweet ment

What has two legs
and two tails?
A dog flipping a coin
What has two legs
and two tails?
A dog flipping a coin

What does a porcupine

eat for dinner?

A sandwich & prickles

What does a porcupine

eat for dinner?

A sandwich & prickles

What is better than a
talking dog?
A spelling bee

What is better than a
talking dog?
A spelling bee

Where do you find a

cat with no legs?

Where you left it

Where do you find a

cat with no legs?

Where you left it

Why can't a
dalmation hide?
They are spotted

Why can't a
dalmation hide?
They are spotted

What kind of cat
has eight legs?
An Octo-puss

What kind of cat
has eight legs?
An Octo-puss

Why could the
dog tell time?

He was a watch dog

Why could the
dog tell time?

He was a watch dog

How do you stop a
bull from charging?
Take his credit card

How do you stop a
bull from charging?
Take his credit card

What should you do
for a blue whale?
Cheer her up
What should you do
for a blue whale?
Cheer her up

Where do sheep get their hair done?

At the baa baa shop

Where do sheep get their hair done?

At the baa baa shop

Why was the bumble
bee's hair sticky?
He used a honeycomb

Why was the bumble
bee's hair sticky?
He used a honeycomb

How do bees get

around town?

On the city buzz

How do bees get

around town?

On the city buzz

What kind of cereal
do cats eat?
Mice krispies

What kind of cereal
do cats eat?
Mice krispies

Why was the

chicken sick?

It had human-pox

Why was the

chicken sick?

It had human-pox

What do you call a

destructive dinosaur?

A T-wrecks

What do you call a

destructive dinosaur?

A T-wrecks

What keeps your teeth
from falling apart?
Toothpaste

What keeps your teeth
from falling apart?
Toothpaste

How do you get a
hot dog to stand?
Take it's chair

How do you get a
hot dog to stand?
Take it's chair

What month has
twenty eight days?
All of them

What month has
twenty eight days?
All of them

What did the baby
light bulb tell his mom?
I love you watts
What did the baby
light bulb tell his mom?
I love you watts

Why did the teacher
wear sunglasses?
She had bright students
Why did the teacher
wear sunglasses?
She had bright students

What letter ends

everything?

G

What letter ends

everything?

G

How do you get on
television?
Sit on it

How do you get on
television?
Sit on it

What has four legs
and can't walk?
A table

What has four legs
and can't walk?
A table

What's easy to get into
and hard to get out of?
Trouble

What's easy to get into
and hard to get out of?
Trouble

What's brown and

sticky?

A stick

What's brown and

sticky?

A stick

What's the hardest
part about skydiving?
The ground

What's the hardest
part about skydiving?
The ground

What do you call a
snowman in spring?
A puddle

What do you call a
snowman in spring?
A puddle

What did one lake
say to the other lake?
Nothing, it waved

What did one lake
say to the other lake?
Nothing, it waved

What can jump

higher than a house?

Anything that can jump

What can jump

higher than a house?

Anything that can jump

What kind of star

is dangerous?

A shooting star

What kind of star

is dangerous?

A shooting star

What kind of music
does grandpa sing?
Pop music

What kind of music
does grandpa sing?
Pop music

Can February
March?
No, but April May

Can February
March?
No, but April May

What did one toilet
say to the other?
You look flushed

What did one toilet
say to the other?
You look flushed

When does B come
after U?

When you steal honey

When does B come
after U?

When you steal honey

Where does a sick
boat go?
To the Doc

Where does a sick
boat go?
To the Doc

Why don't eggs tell

jokes?

They'd crack up

Why don't eggs tell

jokes?

They'd crack up

What nut has
allergies?
A cashew

What nut has
allergies?
A Cashew

What did the teddy
bear say after dinner?
I'm stuffed
What did the teddy
bear say after dinner?
I'm stuffed

When is a baby like

a basketball player?

When she dribbles

When is a baby like

a basketball player?

When she dribbles

What did one bowling
ball say to the other?
I'm on a roll

What did one bowling
ball say to the other?
I'm on a roll

What position does a
ghost play in soccer?
Ghoul-keeper

What position does a
ghost play in soccer?
Ghoul-keeper

Why are hockey
players so cool?
Because of the fans

Why are hockey
players so cool?
Because of the fans

What do you call a
man who exercises?
Jim

What do you call a
man who exercises?
Jim

What do you call a
boy on the wall?
Art

What do you call a
boy on the wall
Art

What do you call a
man with a map?
Miles

What do you call a
man with a map?
Miles

What do you call a

man who owes money?

Bill

What do you call a

man who owes money?

Bill

Who wrote the book

"How to be taller"?

Stan Dupp

Who wrote the book

"How to be taller"?

Stan Dupp

Who wrote the book

"A terrible nightmare"?

Gladys Over

Who wrote the book

"A terrible nightmare"?

Gladys Over

Write your own joke....

Write your own joke...

Write your own joke...

Write your own joke...

Write your own joke...

Write your own joke...

Write your own joke...

Write your own joke...

Write your own joke...

Write your own joke...

Write your own joke...

Write your own joke...

Write your own joke...

Write your own joke...

Write your own joke...

Write your own joke...

Happy Writing!

Manufactured by Amazon.ca
Bolton, ON